Valentine's Day
Dot Markers Activity Book

Ages 2+

With BIG DOT Circles

This book is made to be used with paint daubers or dot markers. Each page has a black background on the reverse to help with bleed-through. Also, you can cut out each page using the trim line or use a separate piece of paper between pages. Have fun!

This book belongs to:
_____

Copyright 2021 Busy Kid Press. All rights reserved.

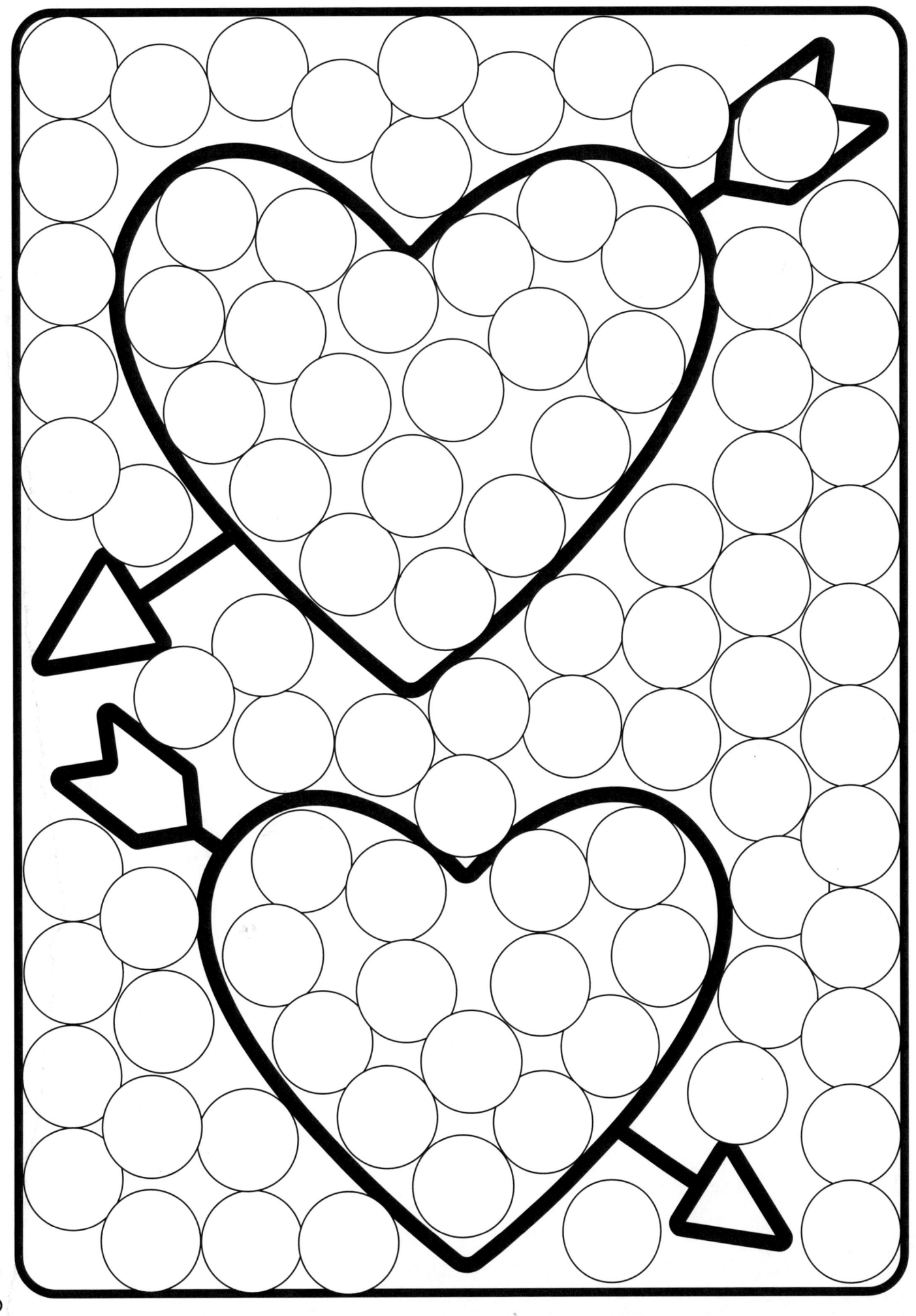

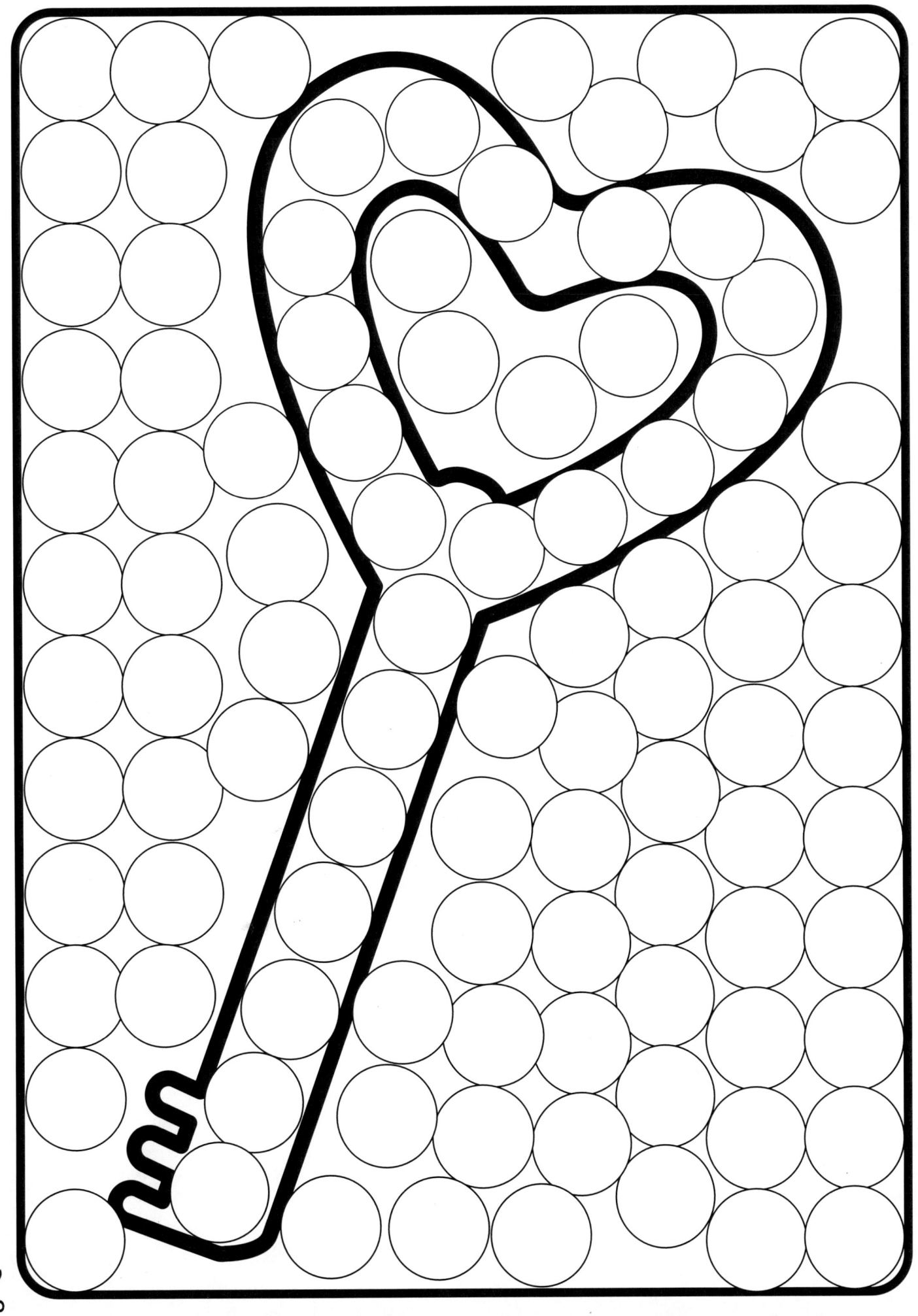

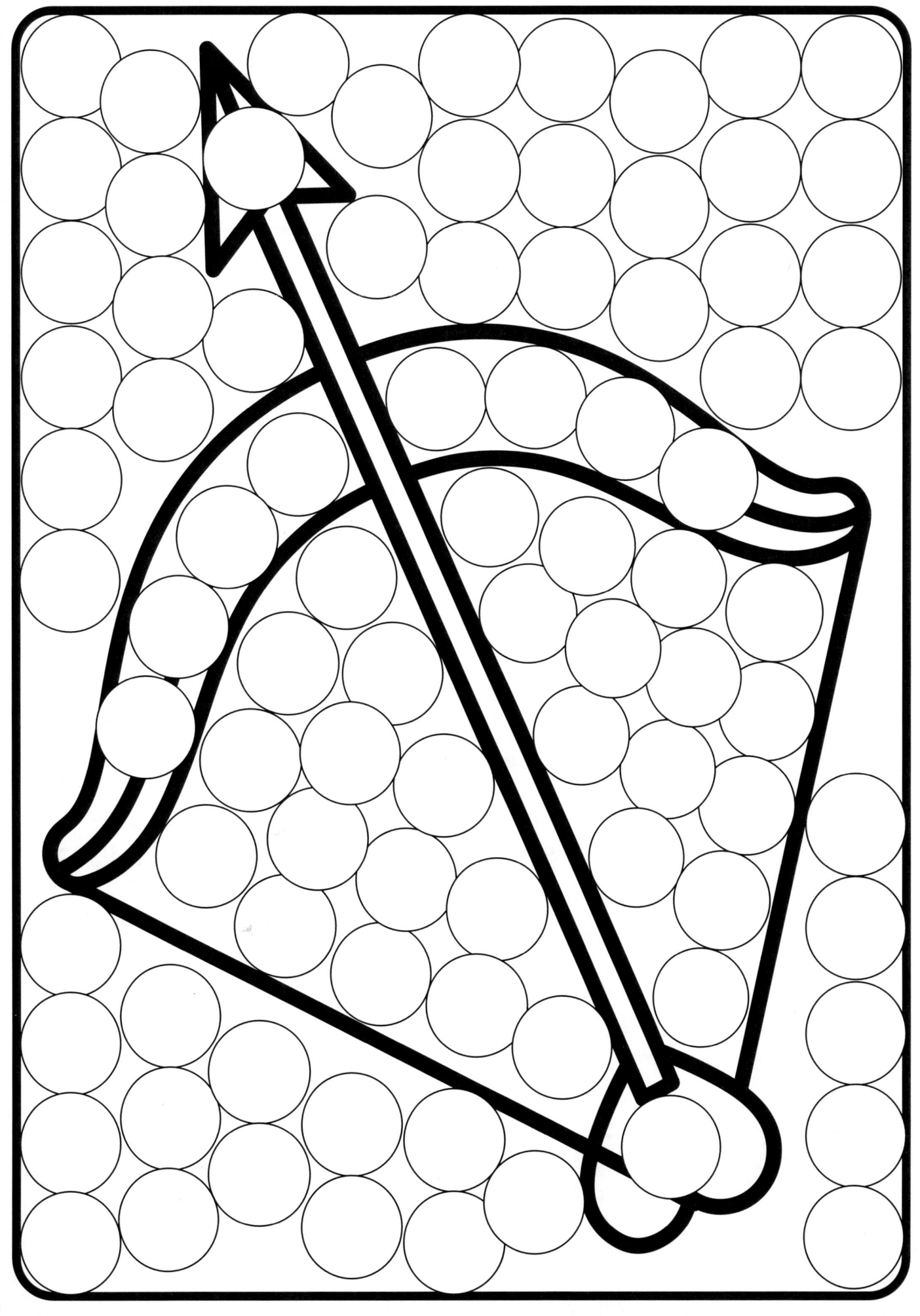

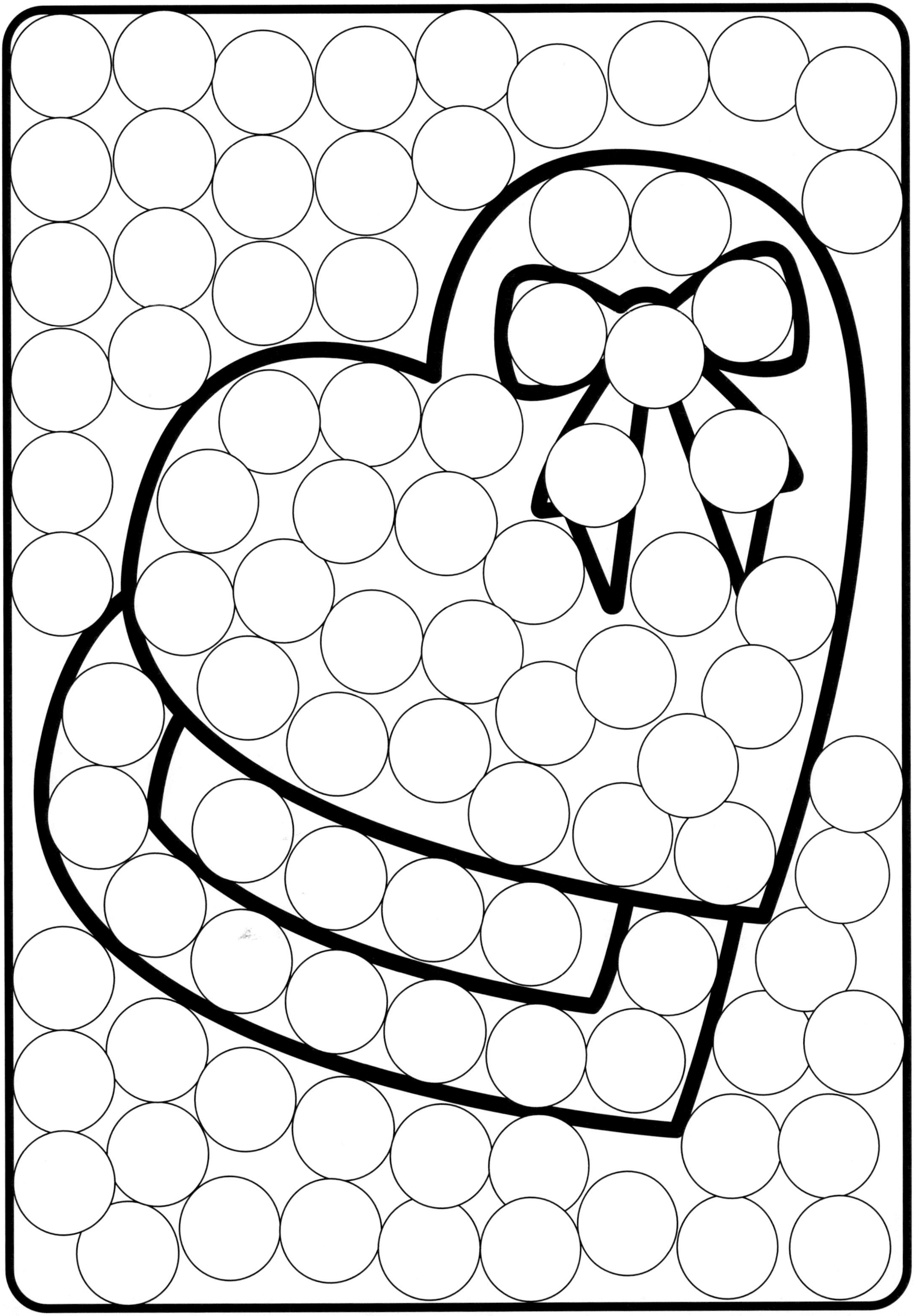

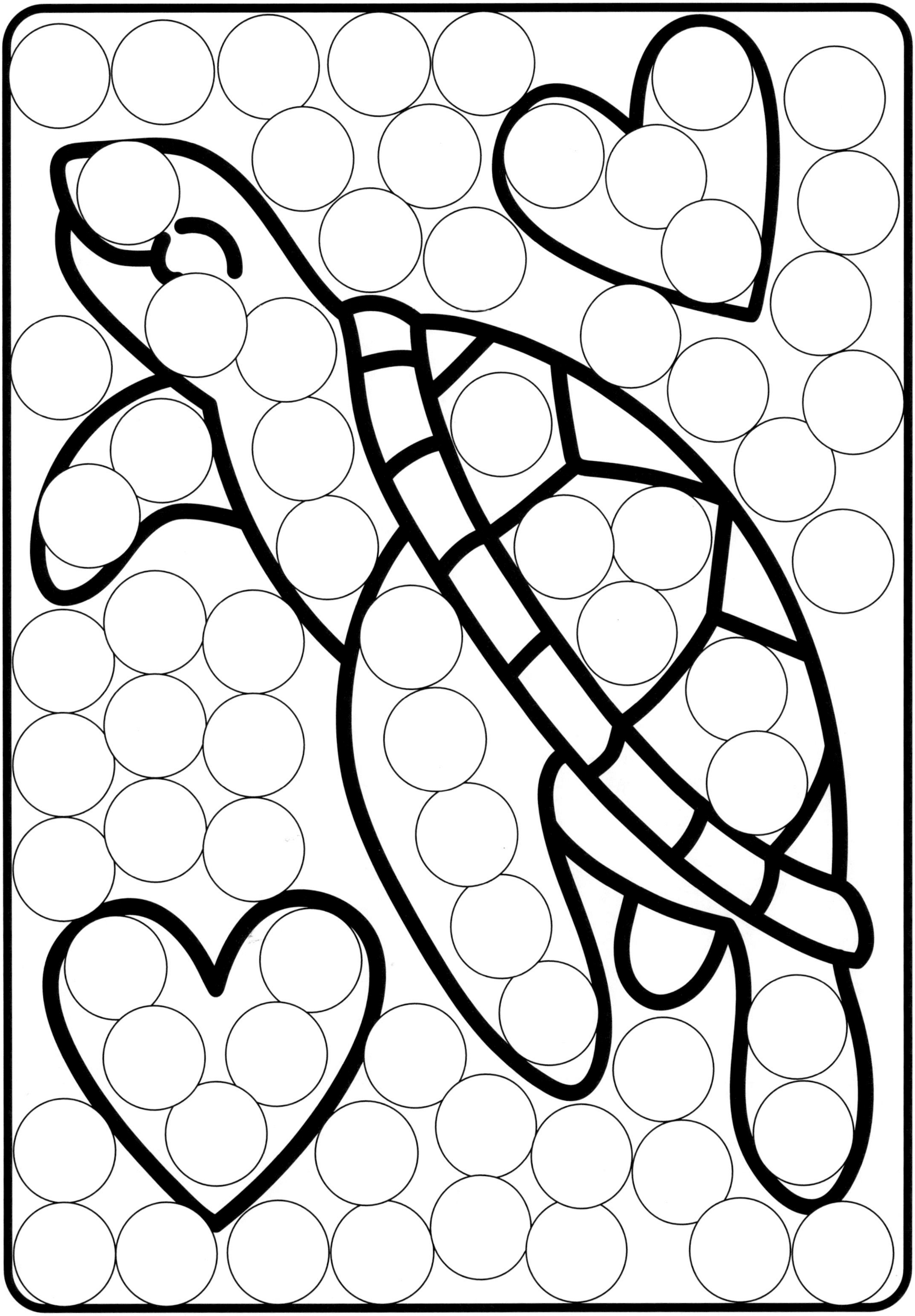

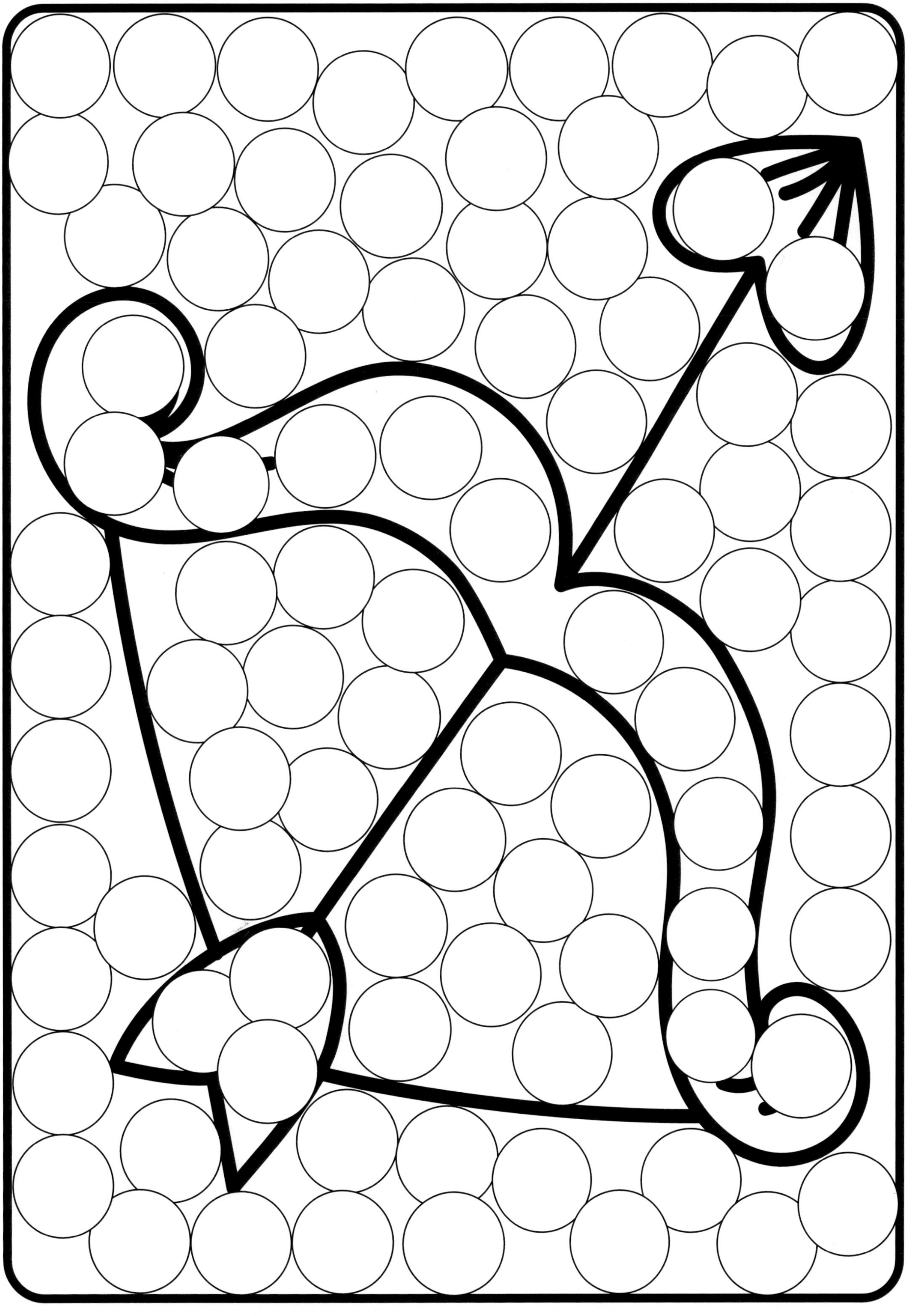

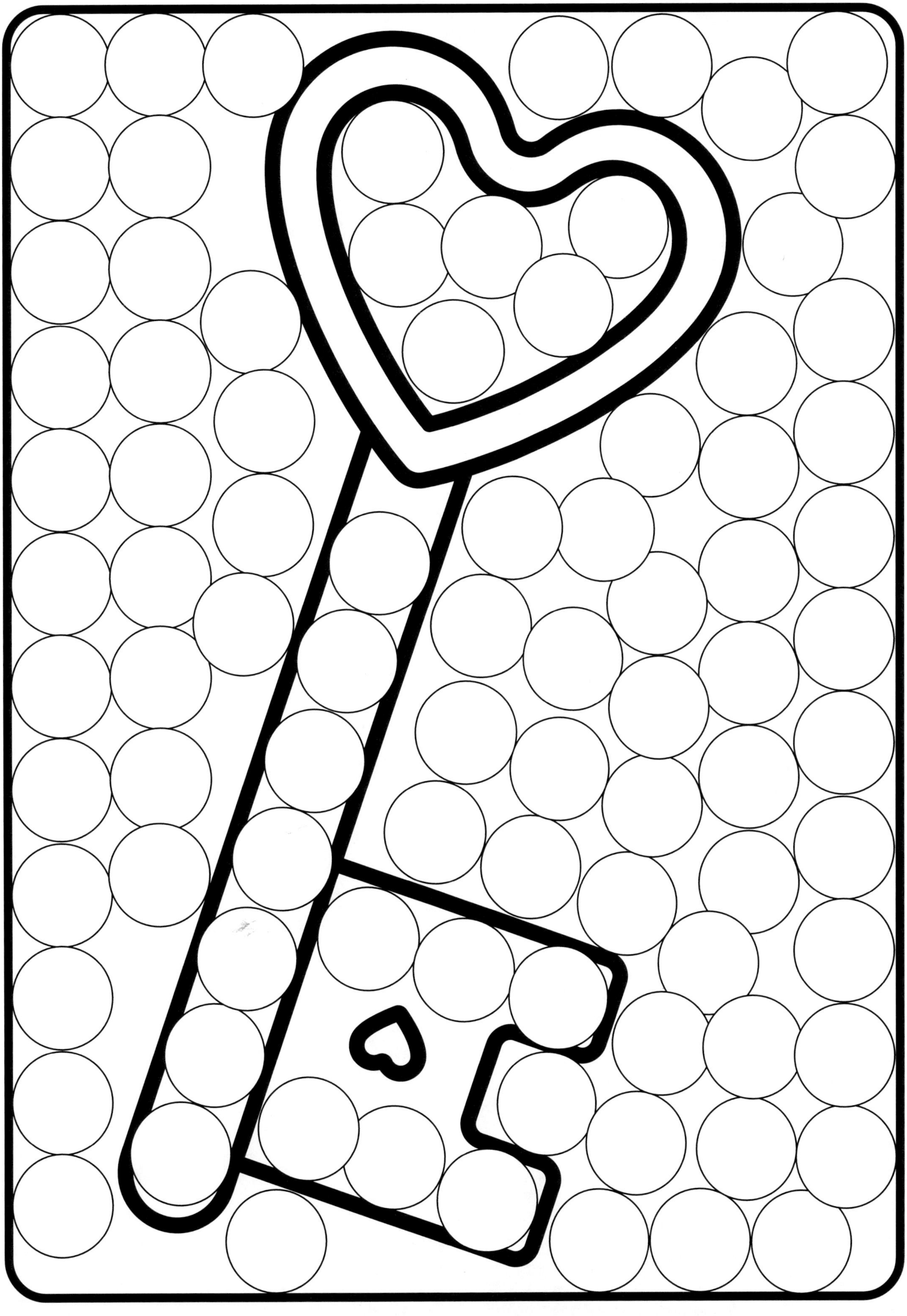

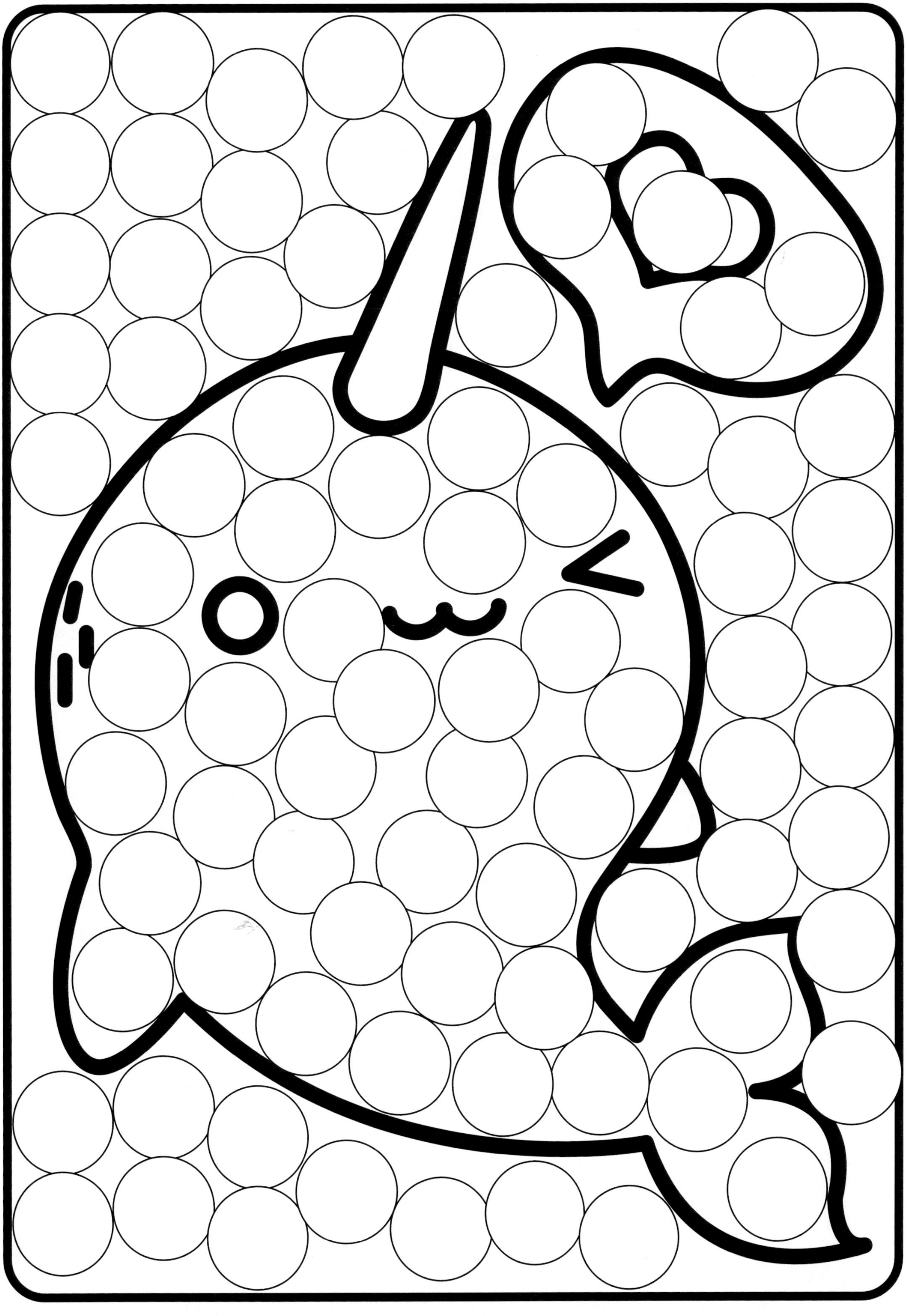

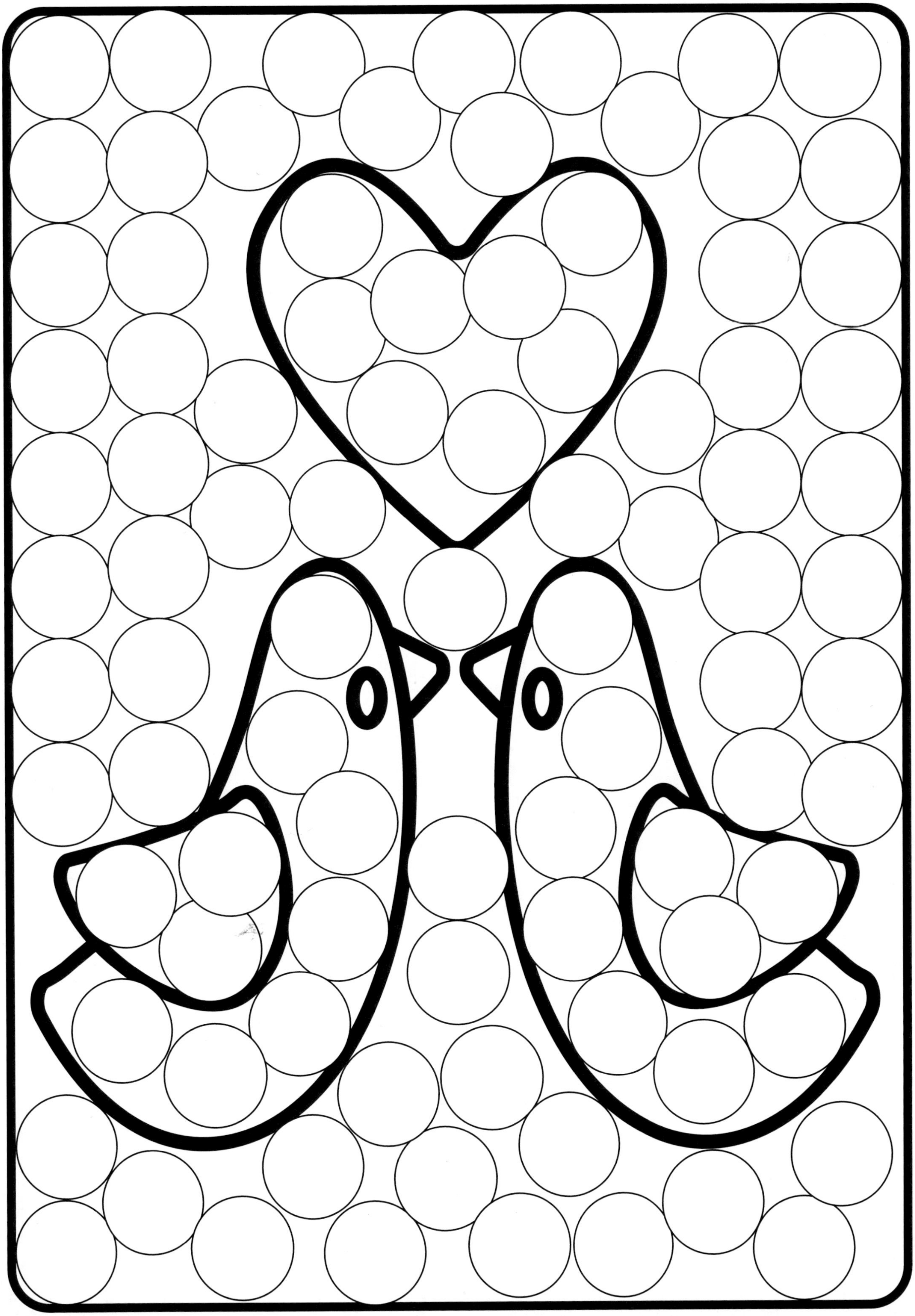

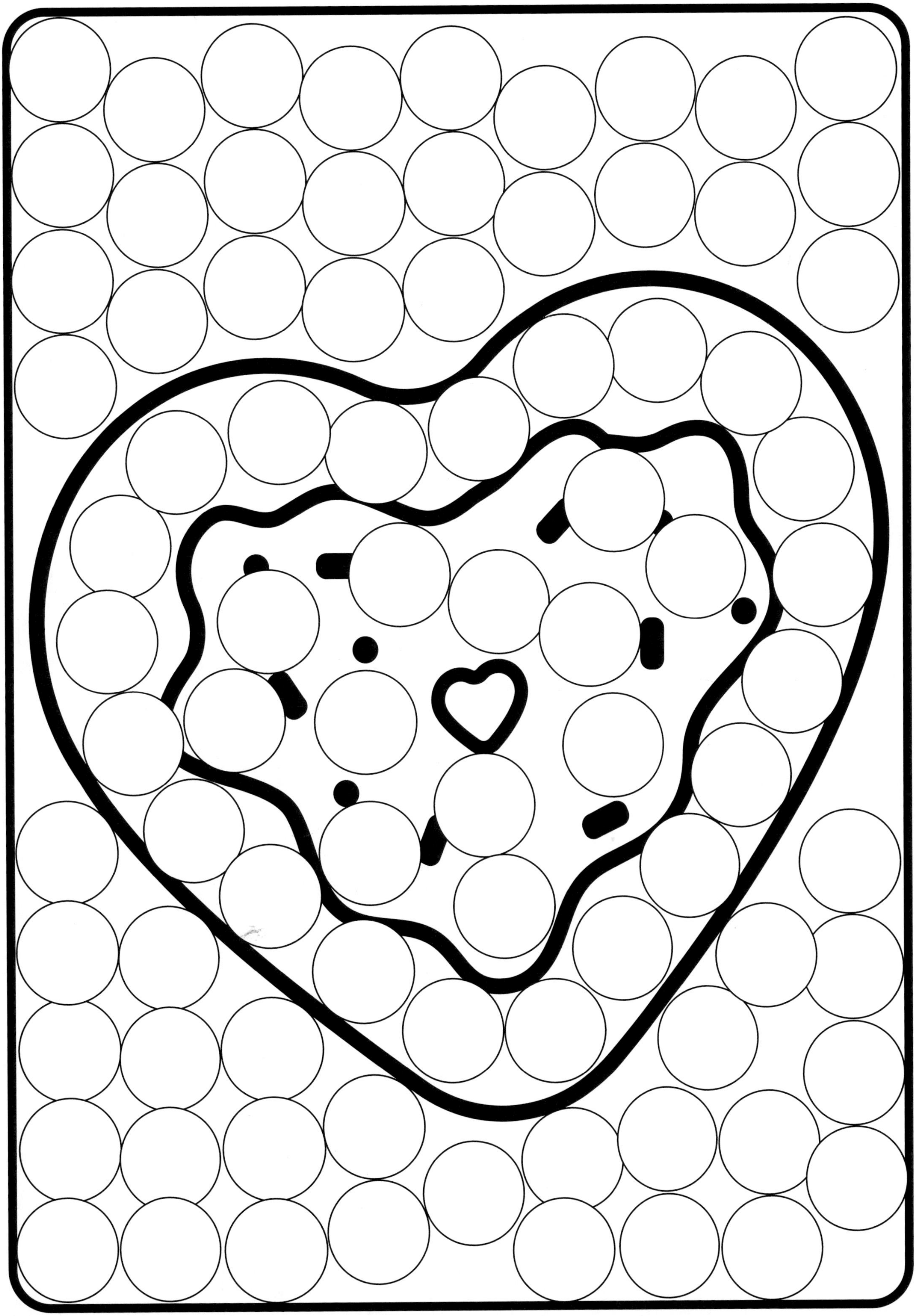

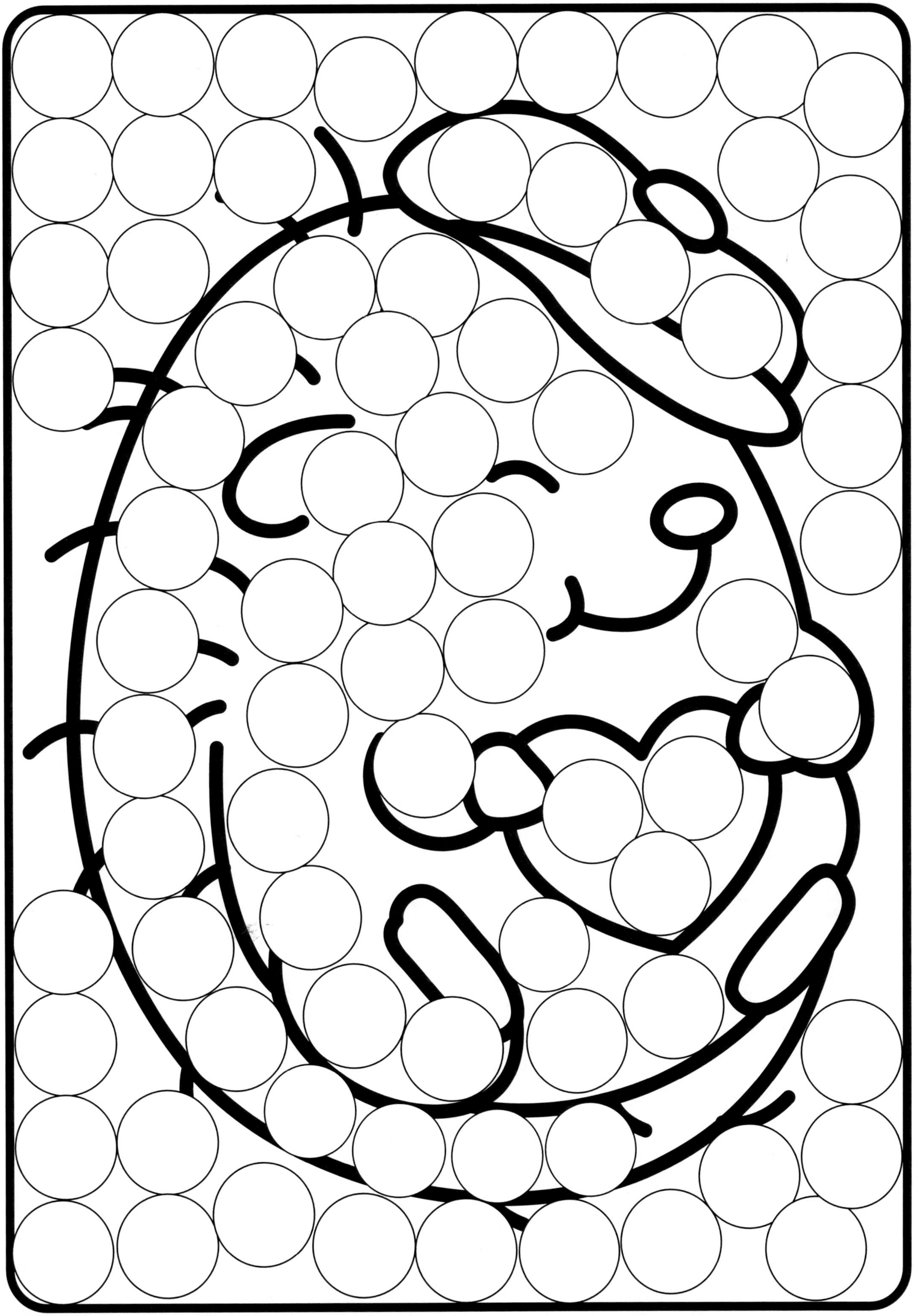

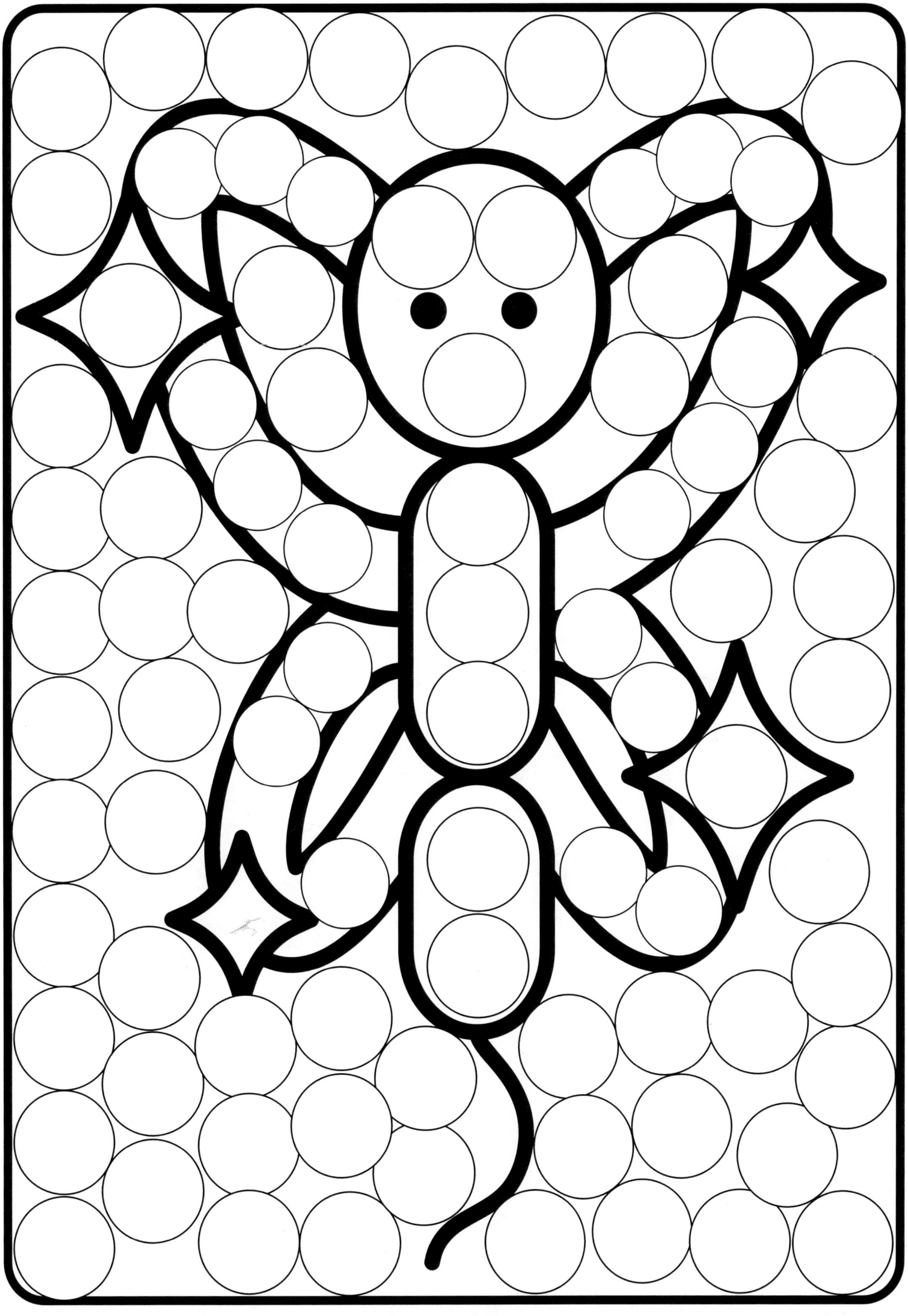

Made in United States
North Haven, CT
03 January 2023